Proof

Elizabeth J. Coleman

Spuyten Duyvil   *New York City*

Library of Congress Cataloging-in-Publication Data

Coleman, Elizabeth J., 1947- author.
 [Poems. Selections]
 Proof / Elizabeth J. Coleman.
    pages cm
 ISBN 978-1-941550-05-2
 I. Title.
 PS3603.O4343A6 2014
 811'.6–dc23

                              2014022342

In memory of my parents, Beatrice and Joseph,
and for my family, Bob, Rachel, Matthew, Kim, Lucy,
Greta, Elliot and Wyatt, with all my love

TABLE OF CONTENTS

1. A Hole in The Sky

2. One Possibility

3. Finally, Justice

4. And I Want to Start Again

"You can never have enough of the world…"
NAZIM HIKMET

I.
A HOLE IN THE SKY

The Bamboo in the Garden

One evening during Sarah's last stay at the hospital, after we told her good night, my best friend and I walked uptown. On our way, we encountered a man standing outside an ethnic deli. He held out a smudged Styrofoam coffee cup. And I reached in my purse for money. *Don't do that*, my friend whispered.

One evening during Sarah's last stay at the hospital, after we told her good night, my best friend and I walked uptown. On our way, we encountered a man standing at an ethnic deli holding an old Styrofoam coffee cup. And I opened my purse for some money. *Don't do that*, my friend whispered. But I had read an article in *The New Yorker* saying that if someone asks you for money, they need it more than you. *This is important to me*, I said. *It's one thing if you have the money out, but don't go fishing around in your purse on the street*, my friend said. I insisted. *Never mind*, the man said.

One evening during Sarah's last stay at the hospital, after we told her good night, my best friend and I walked uptown to find a bit of peace. On our way, we encountered a man standing at one of the ethnic delis that bloom on the streets of New York. He held an old Styrofoam coffee cup in his right hand, as a Buddhist monk in Tibet might hold a begging bowl. And my purse opened, the way a flower unfolds at first light. For I had seen how the world will end, with the fury of water, with daisies and forget-me-nots and even hillsides swept away, and homes tossed into the middle of the road.

Lower Manhattan, September, 2011
For Lance

> *"[A] bird's death leaves a hole in the sky."*
> Z. Herbert

My hairdresser tells me that when he heard
the rumbling, he forgot about his customer
and walked outside, scissors in hand, in time

to see the first plane go in. He tells me
it looked like a cartoon explosion. *I was*
messed up for a while, he says, *but not nearly*

as messed up as friends who lived a block closer,
and saw people not just take off, but land.

I tell him that on that day, we tried
to give blood. But there was no need for blood.

On the radio this morning the Chinese dissident
Yang Maodong, released after five years, didn't
want to discuss hatred or his years of torture.

And now, like banners or Rorschach tests, clouds
float past geometric buildings towards one rising

beneath a crane, this version curved, feminine—
a message to the world that we mean no harm.

4

PRAYER IN ANTICIPATION OF A GUITAR RECITAL

God of small things, big things and everything
in between, help me focus
on my beautiful six-stringed guitar,
so down to earth next to a sinewy violin,
so hearty, like a peasant beside a queen.

Let my ears be
open to it all, so I know
when to be still, when to inhale
like a baby whose belly expands
fully with each breath.

Let me focus on the B
minor key, like a Sherpa
fording a mountain pass who carries
a tourist's load on his back, while he holds
the nervous hiker's hand.

God of all secular Jews who lean
towards Buddhism, give me the skill
and poise to play that elegiac Bach line
with the ease of the Loire running through
a town that brews its own vintage wine.

May this sarabande bow
to the suffering of a parent who has lost a child,
a child a parent, and to the melancholy
Orpheus longing for Eurydice.

Please give me one phrase played
perfectly, just one, like the first
gorgeous shot, by a boy in a ghetto somewhere
who everyone says has no chance.

THE INHERITANCE

My grandfather didn't believe
in reading instructions,

nor do I.
So I married a man who did, and begat

a daughter who does.
I play the guitar but do not care

how it is made,
nor of what wood.

I care only
for what Pepe Romero says:

that every note goes
to the end

of the universe,
and must be beautiful.

My mother was:
silver hair, red lips,

and her pride
in not knowing how

to fix things. My father did,
if asked:

a man who liked
to skip down hotel halls,

and loved computers big as rooms,
the only kind he ever knew.

PROOF

The best proof I've seen that God exists
is found on the face of sand dollars, echinoid fish.
Though it makes me wonder if He used paint by numbers,
the design too charming, unencumbered.

Found on the face of sand dollars, echinoid fish,
a reflection of tern, dune, sandpiper, sky;
a design too charming, unencumbered,
white caps from a Japanese print thunder out of the sea.

A reflection of tern, dune, sandpiper, sky,
my children, young in this picture, skip behind laughing.
White caps from a Japanese print thunder out of the sea.
I want to warn my boy and girl: stay close to me.

My children, young, skip behind laughing.
My daughter's hair flows, undulating sea creature.
I want to warn them: stay close to me;
but want them to break away, dash to the sea.

My daughter's hair flows, undulating sea creature;
my son follows, sweat pants billowing.
I want them to break away, dash to the sea.
The best proof—my children right behind me.

GOOGLE

What lives only for a day? I asked,
and it answered: may-fly, cousin of
the dragonfly, naiad for a year before
it's born, with a mere twenty-four

hours to find someone to love. Whales,
on the other hand, live to eighty-five.
From a rowboat in Baja, Mexico,
I kissed one on its rough back, and I swear

to God, it rolled around, quite pleased.
The elderly priest from Lebanon beside me
on the plane ride home looks up
from translating *The Old Man and the Sea*

into Aramaic, and says, "God wants us
to remain children." So I ask him what
difference it makes whether it's the human
three-score and ten, the whale's eighty-five,

the mayfly's day, or the three years given
to the boy with Taysachs I read about
in the paper whose name means little seal.

LOOKING FOR SYNAGOGUES IN ISTANBUL

Nothing is as it seems in Istanbul,
at least not in tenses that we know.

Does the man who approaches us
in Sultanahmet Square really have
a fiancée in Buffalo? Was the rug seller
up one flight in the bazaar really helping
the weaver's daughter through med school?

I could learn to love this place, the allure
of women in headscarves, something not
revealed, to be revealed.

Cats roam everywhere, a boy ran
through the Blue Mosque, circling
its red carpet. *He's in his home*,
our guide explained.

Making love at dusk, we hear
the muezzins' call to prayer,
watch seagulls—flying minarets—
dive in the Menean Sea. In Turkish,
there's a special tense for dreams.

Everyone wants to help us find
the synagogues, but no one knows
the way. Two workmen on break
lead us through twisted streets

that have no names; the first
synagogue, bland as a suburban home.
A guard house on a shabby street
gives the second one away.

Ten years ago two trucks slammed
bombs into one, then the other:
Bet Israel, Neve Shalom.

Each has a tiny star of David at the top.
In Turkish, there's a special tense for dreams.

BREAKFAST AT SWEET SUE'S

I want to be that little girl,
the one with pink shirt, soft skin, shy smile;
curly hair tied in a lacy bow
at that table, eating a pancake now,
chewing slowly, savoring each bite.

I savor spaces more now,
the shimmering silence between events.
Emptiness no longer scares;
a day of emptiness is best.

"You were going 75,"
the cop says.
Bullshit.
We were dancing, floating, bouncing our way home
from a place with meatloaf and fresh bread.

SOMEONE ALWAYS CRYING IN THE DINING ROOM

Windows closed   diaphanous
curtains unswaying
Before us our words
neatly arranged
on the china   Behind
each a straight-backed chair
Clothes just so   Wine
glasses too small
table-cloth too
white   Stones fell
from our mouths
broke the china

Sometimes my mother
let her napkin drop   ran
from the table and the saddest
Chopin etudes flowed
from her eyes   The door
to the kitchen swung
shut as Marcia—oh, how
I loved her!—went back
to her spicy Jamaican dinner

I want to bolt
through the swinging door
join her in the '50's
kitchen hear her lilting
lime-green laugh the way
she sings her secret
language into the phone to her
sister Yvette or her son
knowing she should be
with them and yet

to have her hold me
close to her enormous bosom
just beyond my reach
under the starched white apron

In Memoriam

I love old-fashioned subway tracks,

Korean churches, exclamation points.

I love to look in other people's homes,

see how they go about their lives.

And love the way a train meanders along.

It's been nine years since the cancer.

I love the deep red of menstruation

and the red of a cut—life made visible,

the body inside out. I miss my period.

Gail died four weeks ago,

a friend who didn't give fake praise

I begged to hear, showed me what

I hadn't seen. A month before, we split

one big Italian meal. Radiant, she wrote down

my son's wedding in her datebook.

ANNA, AGGLUTINATED

Anna's first day back at the convenience store around the corner she gives me a free banana. "Where have you been?" I ask. "Away," she says, coal-black hair in pigtails, a kind of Punky Brewster or Pippi Longstocking look about her.

"No complaints," she answers, when I ask how things are going, each syllable notes apart, as if English were a tonal language. I say the expected: that it doesn't do any good to complain. She loves to complain, Anna laughs, to be heard, since no one ever listened to her as the youngest and smallest of nine. With the air of a winning gymnast, Anna takes twenty-seven cents off the price on a jar of applesauce in my hands.

I ask what they speak back home in Mongolia. Mongolian, she responds and laughs that bell-like laugh. I look up Khalka, the official language, on Wikipedia, and learn it's agglutinative: simple words combined to express compound ideas.

Things are better for me now that Anna's back. When I stop in to buy a banana or a tin of tea, she calls out, "Elizabeth, where have you been?" And summer evenings along Church Street, in solemn rituals, men wheel their food carts back to base, colorful umbrellas closed, aluminum glinting in the evening sun.

A Cup of Tea

It was just a cup of tea
a scrabble game   a mother
two daughters
three full skirts

And on Sundays above Fifth Avenue
Canasta with a Russian
-born grandmother in pink silk pajamas
pouring the brown elixir
through a silver strainer
with a garland border

separating tawny liquid from the leaves
She reminds herself
it's just a cup of tea

It's brown like tans she got
on family trips to Florida by train
Long ago she learned to drink it
white   Her mother had
an English accent

In Malaysian *cha*
the warm mug in her hand
Norwegian word *mug*
simple as a cup or tea

A cousin in the South
has the family samovar
brought from the old country
Russian compound word *samovar*

meaning   boil it yourself
The family from Rakov   Belarus
isolated in a shtetl

Ganeydn Yiddish
for paradise   right now
typing these words
drinking this cup of tea

Skipping Down Broadway

Last night at the restaurant I had an urge to give my meal to the busboy, and let him sip from my oaky chardonnay. Then on the street I wished I were the one who'd handed the guy begging a crisp C-note, like the burly dude in the black three piece suit did. The homeless man skipped down Broadway, telling everyone he passed. And I thought about how someone profiled in *The New Yorker* gave up each of his organs one by one to whoever needed them more.

The Frenchman at the charity dinner tells me: "I already understand that life is meaningless, and I'm just trying to figure out how not to be bored 'til I die." "We give it meaning," I say, and he looks hurt. "Maybe it's a cultural difference, the way we see it," I add. Relieved, he chatters on.

Bastille Day

This morning I could say no
to the wine   to the pills
My highs will be as natural

as Central Park's squirrels
heads up   alert
swishing tails

or the current pushing
that canoe between
New Jersey and New York
with the old couple in it

or Violet the red-tailed hawk
perched on a ledge who turns
her head to the right cleans
a feather   turns
her head to the left
looks up at the sky

If my life is as long as my mother's
I have ten more voyages around the sun
If it's as long as my father's
I have been gone five years

This morning I could be that child
doing somersaults on her front lawn
or a young mother taking her children
for a stroll I could be the sharp smell
of the Long Island Sound or sidewalk
weeds growing through the cracks

I could be a cat licking its paw
or dog peeing good-naturedly
in the bush then trotting on
behind the man with the leash

19, Avenue Franklin Roosevelt

Tears fell on his overcoat
the last time I saw him well,
as my cello and I made our ascent
in 19th Century ascenseur.

The last time I saw him well;
as in a Babar book balloon,
in 19th Century ascenseur,
me in teal-blue mini-dress.

As in a Babar book balloon,
I looked down through the black gate as I rose,
(me in teal-blue mini-dress),
ornate elevator cab barely enclosed.

I looked down through the black gate as I rose
and gray curls, horn-rimmed glasses shrank,
ornate elevator cab barely enclosed.
A doorman had said to the man

with gray curls and horn-rimmed glasses,
Il faut être philosophe dans la vie.
A doorman had said that to the man.
It was to be three months or so

(one must be philosophical in life)
before I grasped the irony,
it was to be three months or so;
but this was where my father left me.

Sometimes I Pass You on the Street

Last night when you jumped
from the bridge into that cold, rough water,
arms flying above loose hair
grown back, full of white,
with that oh what the fuck
attitude some older women have,
you had a great smile and were
wearing terrific lipstick.

I'm wild for the version of "Over
the Rainbow" the way Izzy played it
on his ukelele during the slide-show
of your life, grin present in every shot.
The easy way he sang, disembodied,
on the machine, reminded me of your laugh.

Sometimes I pass you on the street.
Even before you, I would glimpse the others:
Laura and Anne, Judy, hurrying through
the park, purse on one shoulder,
trim briefcase on the other.

What Do Women Want

"What does a woman want?" Sigmund Freud

I want to eat veggie tofu stir-fry and I want to chew mutton bones sucking the
    marrow out of them

I want to tell the doctor in the bowtie who asks me what I do that I'm a lawyer
    at a big firm
and I want to spill red wine on his shirt and tell him I do nothing

To go to a black tie event in high heels by cab
and tromp through Queens in Doc Martens

I want the Mayor to invite me to dinner and I want to picket the Mayor's house

I want to negotiate a climate bill in the Oval Office and to sit in a tree for a year

I want to play the piano like Horowitz and sing in Joplin's lost voice

I want to be driven around Manhattan in a Rolls   and I want to sell sweet corn
off the back of a rusty truck

I want that purse I saw in the window on Crosby Street   and for the world to
be purged of nuclear weapons

I want to bury my face in the pachysandra near my parents' graves   and
I want to see them alive one more time

I would like separate beds please   so I have more space
and I want you to break me in two with your love

I want to reread the Greek Myths   and this time   I want Orpheus
to keep staring   resolute no matter what   at the sunrise straight ahead

2.
ONE POSSIBILITY

MIDDLEFIELD

Barns collapse in graying fields;
old men have stopped their milking now,
a sigh for what their brown land yields,
barns collapse in graying fields.
You sense a bit how their grief feels,
a sidelong glance at aging cows.
Barns collapse in graying fields,
old men have stopped their milking now.

Twilight click of horses' heels
tells of Amish passing by:
blue frocks, black caps, two large spoked wheels,
twilight click of horses' heels.
They've made their peace with graying fields,
curtains drawn for privacy.
Twilight click of horses' heels
tells of Amish passing by.

There once were daily home-baked pies
for men returning from the fields,
strawberries picked by aproned wives.
There once were daily home-baked pies.
Brick homes will replace barns and sties
as old men's children make their deals.
There once were daily home-baked pies
for men returning from the fields.

Beyond a Reasonable Doubt

You always plead the fifth.

On a farm—
too much fancy interferes with milking.

You won't confess, but your eyes
proffer evidence, the way they crinkle
in the corners when I give my testimony:

I first loved you beyond a reasonable doubt,
not when you stood in the Great Hall at Penn Law
in moss-colored v-neck looking thin and out of place.

No, it was that time in the parking lot.
You touched my neck—on our way
to buy Mike's wedding present—that touch
corroboration of something more.

This is the plea I cop: once we began
there were no bars, no demurrers, no disputes of fact.
When I saw the wallpaper flowers in the room
where your sisters used to sleep,

habeas corpus, my love.
"So when do you want to get married?"
Your opening statement.
"Because of Apartheid, I can't give
you a diamond ring."

The party of the second part wore a long Indian gown
& glasses, concentrating on her torts textbook. She looked up,
didn't need a closing argument.

As proof, she milked her first cow.

BODDHAVISTA

They flocked to see the mystic,
prayed for answers. She said I do not
know better than you;
I only know to keep my gaze
still, perfume
natural; to treat
my thoughts less
like a town crier than
a listing boat on a river.

Her funeral was packed
with Christian, Muslim,
Hindu, Jew,
even a Bahai gentleman who
liked the smell of incense,
her long red hair, big breasts;
that she never said
things happen for a reason,
understood the randomness of love.

CUMBERLAND ISLAND

Live oaks wear Spanish moss
the way flamenco dancers
add scarves or earrings.

Remember how we danced where
waves come in, threaded shells
along hoop earrings, ran across dunes,

then dove in—seaweed soft as moss—
swimming with the grace of dancers
in velvet sea of blue and green?   Now

I walk along the shore, by earringed oaks
of many arms: Bodhisattva dancers sway
towards decaying mansions by the sea.

Primeval green canopy beckons me to take
a bike from the old barn, ride past magnolia
leaves, across roads and sand, hair, necklace,

earrings flying to the sea. Fiddler crabs, contra dancers,
sidle up, sideways; oyster catchers and terns wade in
anticipation. Wild horses repose, hooves caressing sand.

And conch wrings an oboe's song as I divine the sea.

CENTRAL PARK

On Poet's Walk, the lone saxophonist
belts out a standard I heard years ago.
My father played it on the piano,
in a red jacket, daring at the time.

I pass toy boats on the pond
like one he guided in his pool;
at Strawberry Fields think of John
Lennon's short time on earth, and
dad's, the latter not well known.
It's small consolation that his signet ring
I've worn forty years will become my son's
and survive by many generations
strewn trash that floats, slovenly,
among the park's gold-tinted leaves.

ANNUAL PHYSICAL

Vilma has an accent like my grandfather's.
He and I watched *Lassie* Sunday nights until
the doctor said all that emotion was bad
for his heart. Sometimes I wonder about life

in the shtetl, think of Chagall's people and houses
floating, unmoored, wonder if my family loved
to bicker even then. Vilma, not Wilma—there's no
"W" in Lithuanian, she tells me—dresses simply.

My grandmother wore a silk suit, ruby earrings,
matching brooch, and I remember the ice's clink
in her *wodka*, as she called it. I wear dangly earrings,
and overdo it, my mother says. "Less jewelry

would be better. Get all dressed up, then remove
one accessory," she instructs. Vilma tells me
to pee in a cup. When a New Jersey policeman
ordered my grandmother to sweep the snow

off her sidewalk, she moved to New York, or so
the story goes. As Vilma takes my blood, weighs me,
does an electro-cardiogram, she announces,
"It's a *wonderful city*," enunciating the W with a care

that reminds me how my grandfather used to fold
the American flag on summer nights, the way he taught me
never let it drop.

THE FAMILIAR

For Claude

And yet I could not tutoyer the Breton nun,
that needed an ease beyond my ken;
or the man whom I desired,
or the farm town he came from.

Because Mulberry has two Chinese funeral homes,
a *Daily News* wind-blown against the park,
thick steam swirling from every block,
New York I tutoie you.

Grayness descends, drapes buildings, dresses them;
it's more a Paris than a New York day,
a place I once could tutoyer.

These days I hesitate to say "tu" too fast;
something about vous makes feelings last.

AT THE FUNERAL OF MY FATHER-IN-LAW OF FORTY YEARS

On Sundays the minister spoke of rooms with flowered
wallpaper, where the saved would one day live in the sky
with Jesus, and the organ and piano play hymns out of tune

and sync, as I was out of sync and tune with what was said
from time to time within these walls. Now Samantha asks
where *I* think her grandfather is, and I say I don't know,

suddenly as sure in my not knowing as she is in her certainty—
and she becomes the first person I will ever tell
about my cousins shot in a synagogue in Rakov, Belarus.

This is the room where I put my arm around my father-in-law
Christmas Eve, the year he turned ninety-three, as he leaned
into me, trembling on a crooked cane, singing softly to his Lord.

THE WAY I FEEL FOR YOU

round and white, a full moon
over the Sandia Mountains
on a blue September night, round,
and pure white, light imagined
by one without sight.

Above a fence near the Rio Grande,
I see it, a ball of white,
in bas-relief
this sharp fall night.

The globe's suspended,
a child's kite, sky blue written
with a fountain pen,
paper alone where the moon is white.

My chill increases towards
midnight, as kite of moon
makes its descent;

suspended,
a child's kite, sky blue filled in
by a fountain pen,
without you, this
still Sandia night.

The First Time

There is a blue plaid kilt

There is a bed with clean sheets

There are two drops of blood

that are the red of the first time

of the tinge in eyes that have cried

of stoplights that dot my city

of ladybugs my mother always

said were good luck   of a scratched

mosquito bite   a holly bush the red

of the bra Judy Stein wore

under a white blouse one day to school

It was shocking at the time

The Gesture

He and I have been fighting again in that dull way
as we run down the subway's filthy steps. On the N
we're squeezed close by the crowd. "I don't understand

his accent." an elegant woman next to me says about
the disembodied voice on the loud-speaker. "Is it
Arabic?" "Just New York," I laugh. "Williams, I love

him." She points to my book. "It's like a Haiku; like
he's made an oriental painting," and she pens a stroke
in the air with her hand. "A gesture," I suggest. "Yes,

a gesture," she says, with a beautiful accent I can't place.
"His poems are supple as a dancer's steps," I say, understanding
suddenly how looked at in a certain way, everything is

calligraphic. Doors open at 14th Street, and the crowd floats
forward. Above ground, foil from a crinkled chewing gum
wrapper someone has thrown down reflects back the warmth

of the sun, so I take his arm as we walk to the restaurant
where we've arranged to meet our son.

LET'S

hang out in a Bearden collage
yellows   African prints   bright blues
sharper edges to our bodies

Let's plop onto a Pollock canvas
ochre green or black
bop to tenor sax's voice
as we tumble down

and chew our cuds in a Corot
gaze out on all the people wandering by
who'll admire our tawny hides
They won't see the flies

form staccato notes in a Bartok piece
jagged   dissonant   Let's appear
here and here and here   please

Let's hover on the ceiling at Grand Central
in lime green as we memorize
the constellations
savor Swahili   Portuguese
Tagolog of passers-by

Let's make love in a Garcia-Marquez book
while parrots chatter in the courtyard
and we reinvent the world
round as a naranja

ILLUMINATION

Only when I began to study art,
did I see the way light falls on fruit,
how much of an apple is blue, not red
in the sun, or that there are spots
so luminous they're best represented
by the blank page. I didn't understand
that art is illumination, and to appreciate
a Pissarro, you have to see the way
the rays come through the trees into brown
wood. So too, really to see your child
who cleverly plucked some features from you
and some from your husband to create her own
astonishing face, you must look
at the way light falls on those green eyes.

ON CONTEMPLATING MY MORTALITY
For Myra and David

Since pigeons count and sparrows
mourn their dead, and it's lovely

to run into someone we'd never go out
of our way to see, the least I can do is stop

eating things with eyes. In my dream, my father:
alive, mellow and curious about these past

forty years. Buddhists know not to take it all
personally. I'm trying to stop taking green pills

to sleep from fear of the one for eternity.
Last week someone I admire asked me to consider

an alternative to nothingness. And, for his sake,
I pictured a tiny opening, like an elf's door in a tree

or even smaller, a doll-house door. I remembered
the Matisse painting where a round-headed man

stands in the middle of the room, and light
comes flooding in from both sides.

A Daughter Looks to Fir Mountain

The porch protects the house from cold,
the way I said I'd shut my heart to you.
But the door blew open; now I see

my mountain loom. Your laughter was
a Buddhist bell calling the monks to prayer
and your wit was mountainous.

On summer nights I open all the windows—
from my room I hear Esopus flow. And if I rise
before first light, I see her:

arms folded, not unlike a mother,
bossy against the sky.

ONE POSSIBILITY

I wonder if that mother baboon in Tanzania is out on the rock
with her infant savoring the evening sun. That's how it is:
one day you're sitting on a ridge holding your child, thinking

it doesn't get better than this, the next, it could be you people are calling
about: did you hear? She was so young and *in medias res.* But aren't we all,
except maybe the cellist Casals, who at ninety announced he was done,

or my father-in-law when helping with the barn-cleaner was too much.
If souls really transmigrate, maybe I'll come back as an eland. I fell in love
with the one in the Serengeti, whose eyes signaled it knew it would die

that night. Puss ran from his nose, and he didn't have the energy to run
from us. Homeless people die on the streets of New York from the cold
all the time. I wonder if it's human nature to admire the rich, how clean

they are, how sure, and to rush past people who live in cardboard boxes,
annoyed at thoughts being interrupted, threatened by their need,
forgetting any one of them could be Jesus testing us.

3.
FINALLY, JUSTICE

Finally, Justice

I used to have a country-song love of the open road,
back when I married for the love of civil rights, for
the love of a farmer's boy who loved that road, when
we were from Atlanta and lawyers for the poor, and
painted my office lavender, when the children were
young, before cars were air-conditioned and the world
was burning up, so we'd roll down our windows, and
didn't mind sweating, hair blowing behind us like
Thelma and Louise before they sped off the cliff,

and we drove where wild horses fed on sea oats grass, past
towns built on sand, where reclaimed couches and seized
homes backlit magnolias' brash blooms, back when you
were trying to keep Warren McClesky from being
executed for a white cop's death, and Warren maintained
his innocence: that disarming smile, white jail garb
on a man who'd found Jesus, become a prison preacher.

Back then, we counted on the heat smell, the way we drove
in South Georgia for days past the Okefenokee's mangrove
swamps, its trees with stout trunks like a child's sturdy legs,
past our past, past little towns where I was sure being a lawyer
would be romantic, and there would be a storefront and a wooden
sign with my name on it across from the ante-bellum courthouse.
And this time, I swear, we will save Warren.

SAUDADE

As an umbrella doesn't cause the rain
a mailbox doesn't write the letter
and rain doesn't cause my longing

this morning when we made love
I was half asleep
and desire didn't awaken

fast enough though love did
But love is not compassion
just as kindness is not art

I tell the woman with sculpted curls
behind the counter that when I saw her
on the subway I wondered where I knew her from

Oh how I'll miss the Post Office
and mailboxes on every other corner
covered in graffiti   knowing when

my letter will leave   Picturing that
moment of delivery
and the one of opening

At a Café Overlooking a Tenth-Century Church, Eril-le-Val, Spain

For K.M.H.

Someone will hand me a guitar and I'll play
Spanish songs for you by heart. And we won't be
Americans of late middle age, but mythic creatures
who have lit down in this ancient place. There will be
a timelessness, as in a film whose sound-track
is a sole guitar. And that moment will contain every one
where you and I have cried or laughed together
over stories no one else will ever know, one reference
leading to the next and next, then wending its way
back through time to when we met, day one
of law school, shy of each other as one is
in that first mysterious encounter.

For your words have been my shade all
these years from 3, 000 miles away, words
on legal pads in your competent, bold hand,
words spoken through phone lines as I sat in the bath,
words typed on emails now, but still that shade,
made by the delicate tree of your words.

GEORGE WASHINGTON BRIDGE

I watch the red umbrellas down below
merged in mist with people passing through.
I can't shake the sadness of the rain;
a grayness has submerged the streets again.

Not a downpour that prevails on you
to run for shelter, laughing with a friend
dashing arm and arm down subway stairs.
No, one that invites you to feel alone,
dwell on acts for which you've not atoned.

But I made amends, I tell myself.
After all, I came back to this town
to be close to where my mother lies
and to the small red lighthouse beneath
the grand gray bridge she lovingly
described each time that we passed by.

Where Exactly Is Heaven in Relation to the Sun?

There's a Russian Jewish shoemaker on our block, the place dirty, also a barbershop. He barely speaks English, throws the shoes around with no respect, but they come back good as new. One day as I left, he said, "I love you, honey." You could tell he thought it was something people say here just to be friendly. In lucky moments, I'm sure heaven is wherever this is: a shop, an airplane with plastic seats, a train car that smells of urine, for that matter. Last week on the Long Island Railroad, the conductor, cap at a rakish angle, told the guy next to me. "I got you yesterday." "How do you know it was me?" he asked. "Every conductor has a different punch," she said. I noticed the distinct hole on my ticket. Each snowflake with its own pattern, all zebras with singular stripes, a giraffe's spots one of a kind, now this. "I had no idea," I said. "That's why I carry index cards in my pocket," the conductor explained. "There's always something new to learn; and I note it down." She pulled them out with a flourish, yet with care, and I thought of African countries where lines snake around as people wait to vote for days, they care so much. Then this morning for a moment, listening to the radio, I considered converting to Islam in solidarity, like the young Germans who converted to Judaism after the War.

TICKER-TAPE PARADE
For Marie Ponsot

"In war, fathers bury their sons."
Herodotus

At 10 am I cheered the crowd at the Giants'
Ticker Tape Parade. But now it's noon,

and they could be clamoring for blood,
my blood. I could be in Liberia, at risk

of being shot by someone young enough
to be my grandchild. A mob can turn

any time, they say. What I admire about
the Giants' parade is there are no

distinctions among people, The only rules:
that you love NY, which I do, and football

which sadly I cannot. Though it's only
in my later years I've come this far, now

that World War II is history. Since high school
my favorite quote from Herodotus about how

it's one thing for a child to lose a parent, but
then to see the video of the twenty-seven year old.

On the football field he was meant to run right,
but the hole wasn't open so he cut and ran through.

Sometimes he dreams he's driving, he says.

ROMANCING BASEBALL

I've never seen the lure
of sports, except haphazardly.
Last night, above Shea stadium, the sky,
lit by a three-quarter moon, turned
the ink blue black of Van Gogh's cafe scene
over the diamond on the green expanse,
me ensconced between husband and son,
baseball their true romance. When it came time
to stand for Take Me Out, grown men arose—
not worrying how it seemed—they smiled,
put down their beers and sang, boys of five again.
I cheered and chomped on pizza with congealed cheese
on top, reeled in by the nostalgic frieze.

FOR NINE MONTHS

I dreamed every night you were fine,
fingering pearls with polished nails.
Mornings I woke, refreshed.

Mother, you would have felt so impolite
to die on my birthday; to-do list in pocket;
Bargello tapestry half done.

Sometimes in a dream
I give birth to you, vodka in hand,
laugh high like the clink of glasses,

twirling your wrist to make a point.
When, from time to time, I conjure you,
it's the best I know how to do.

BREATHLESS

She never had much taste for virtue,
liked her cinema noir, vrai—
blouses tight, striped across small breasts—.
wore jeans with heels before all the rest.
Disdained herb teas à l'Américaine;
smoked little brown cigars that went with scotch,
sans rocks, and bitter dark espressos
at the bar, in Paris when it was still
Parisien; a place piano players
might get shot walking down the street, and,
breathless, Jean-Paul had Jean
until he died, in hails of bullets.
Où sont les cigarettes d'antan? she cried.
We'll always have the Tribune, he replied.

Dividing Lines

In the middle
of the day it sidles in
the sense I matter as little
as the moth struggling
in that spider's web

but then I remember
the bumper sticker
on a VW Beetle that announced
kindness is my religion and decide again

to be a vegetarian and apologize
to the spider I accidentally
washed down the drain
and save the ant in spite
of its wily self that's avoiding
the store receipt I'm using
as a stretcher to ferry it outside
to safety so I press a stem
of broccoli into service in its stead

O Violão

My mother and I were large
on the bottom, small on top,
like guitars. *What they admire
in Brazil*, Tim said.

Sometimes on the radio you hear
a singer from the 30's on a scratchy
old record. That's how she sang,

high voice, English accent,
embarrassed by her old-fashioned
sound, but proud too. I sat under

the piano, listened, watched. She was all
curves and had the tenderness of a falling leaf.
How I long to call her on one of those

telephones with curly black wire.
But all I have is my guitar: I put her
on my leg, strum so mother will hear:

forte   sul tasto
guitar's eye open
mine closed.

THE LITTLE BOY

After *The Piano Lesson* by Henri Matisse

Ancient metronome
shaft of light
triangle shape
boy's face
more surprised
than happy

Who would be happy
with a disembodied
woman in the room?
The piano teacher has no breasts
and her stool is just a sketch
a gray stroke to show

blouse and skirt
For God's sake
let her be real
or go away

Window open
green spring day
How can he listen
to Bach's invention?

Madame, can I go out and play?
But he loves how the curves
on the balcony match the ones
on the Pleyel stand

Curve to curve
Triangle to triangle
Rectangle to rectangle
Orange to orange
blue to blue
as he too
disappears

The Subway Car

After the surgery, Dr. Dottino said, someone
just handed you thirty years, and I remember what
held my unborn children, feel the absence inside me.

In the Serengetti, a mother baboon sat on a rock
under an acacia tree, held her infant in her arms
at end of day. An elephant and her calf fed ten feet away.
Ears unfurled like four rolls of Italian marble paper.

In a subway car strewn with papers, guitar
strapped on like a child riding piggy-back,
off to play for patients at my hospital, a stranger says,
my son Steven studied guitar in Seville. He looks
embarrassed and bored, and I envy his youth, regret
I began the things I care for so late, wonder if I've made
good enough use of this gift, one third now gone.

I want to care for the animals in the Bush the way
I tended to my children, shield the wildebeest
from crocodiles and the dying eland who let us
come close, stare into his eyes, from the lions,
and the lions and elephants from us.

Subway acrobats somersault across the dirty car.
A street preacher with an African accent shouts:
open your eyes, there are 1,001 reasons why
you should pray today!   A pregnant woman
in cowboy boots next to me plays
mahjong on her I-phone.   I love it,
she tells me, smile beatific.

A Beautiful Day for a Funeral

Funny when I cry and when I don't,
Ellen says walking into the chapel.
You knew my dad so well. But I'd never
heard how at seven he caught
a fly ball near third and won a trophy
or how he was once mistaken
for a homeless man. He was two years

younger than my mother would have been
if she'd had another twenty years. *It's a big deal
to be an orphan*, I tell Ellen. *It hasn't sunk in,*
she says. On the subway home, a man with sunken
eyes and dyed rodents on his shoulders bears a sign:
*For pictures, tips appreciated. Are they guinea pigs
or rats?* I ask the woman across the aisle. *Rats,*
she says with great authority, *they have long tails,*
and she laughs loud enough to wake the dead.

The Open Road

Slim and shy and farmer's-son kind
in light green v-neck sweater and jeans,
a restive energy in your stride, you smiled
at a description of Passover in a bar,

astride a chair, mustachioed face,
pull of country in your mien,
straight nose, hair wild as tumbleweed.

That spring I watched your forward lean
into mustard Camaro's gallop, heading
for the open road. He'll never love
a city girl, I thought.

Three decades since we first met
I squint across the years
to find that silhouette.

Gauguin's Words

"Que sommes-nous? Où allons-nous?" Paul Gauguin

Leaf shadow strums the sidewalk etched in gray,
asking, "Où allons nous?" Run before
it's too late; away from this town and its small store
that sells only buttons and will seduce
a farmer's son. It's not the leaf we miss,

but the shadow, and tag games of tow-headed children.
Like the woman in the film who never delivered
the letters, I long even for those I loved

poorly, old boyfriends, cigarettes dangling
from cynical mouths.

Admission Against Interest

Let the record reflect:
ab initio, that first law school year,
I chose; you demurred
(no defamation intended).
Sua sponte, duces tecum.

Let's expunge from the record
failures of consideration; we've held one
another harmless,
the elements of enchantment elusive,
an act of God.
Sua sponte, duces tecum.

A plea: after my statute of limitations
has run, my rule against perpetuities
played out, when I've lost all appeals,
you'll still be at counsel table, by my side.
Sua sponte, duces tecum

SERENADING THE PATIENTS IN THE ICU
Memorial Sloane Kettering Cancer Center

You can go in, the nurse said, warm, professional,
kind. "His father's in there with him," she said.

I thought I could bear suffering until I saw that man
without a face, a man younger than my children.

Well, no, the face was there, but skin where an eye
should be, where part of a nose, part of a mouth should be.

I tried to act normal. "Would you like some music?"
But he shook his head. *Time Magazine* hung from

the father's hand. I tried to walk away slowly
from where one man sat in a chair and one lay

in a hospital bed, the wrong one
in the chair, the wrong one in the bed.

WE TRY TO TALK BUT DON'T KNOW WHAT TO SAY

After Muriel Rukeyser

Snow fell on the stone wall, like a sonata
or the mourning sound of a crow,
or a head against a mother's shoulder.

Say something, anything. I want to know
what you're doing, each moment, as I go
about my day.

When my father played *Laura* by ear
on the piano, you could tell he was talking
to my mom. He never lived the life he wanted.

Hold me.   Cup my breasts.   Who are you?

Trying not to tell me how ill he was,
Bursitis, they said.

But the black wires gave them away.
It took the operator an hour to set up the call.
Phone lines slithered along the ocean floor.

If morning light hadn't shone pink over
its wings, the plane home
could not have borne the sadness.

Say something, anything.

CATSKILLS LOVE

Mornings   you look old   a bit
like your father but I don't
mind just as you don't seem to mind
that as usual my life is
in disarray   the way the picture
we got in Quito of the South American
sky with the clouds that are all
the same   is crooked on the wall
or that untamed look in my eye first thing
and that my hair grays as you gaze

outside   where   the orange
of a monarch butterfly clashes
with a purple bearded iris
forget-me-nots on the hill remind
me of the last tufts of hair
on a balding man

So come inside   and while there's time
let's make our bodies
one like those jigsaw puzzles
your mother loved to put together
on the card table while she watched
tv in color

ELEGY

If I were a foreign country, I'd be Spain,

not France, for the duende of it. And

if I were France, I'd be Brittany

with its rocky shore, feisty politics,

Gaelic sounds, cone-shaped hats

that no longer exist, except in Gauguin's

paintings or at pageants.

He loved jazz and the stride

pianist Cliff Jackson he'd once heard,

but was afraid to fly, the way life

skirts the edge of death, and

jazz and duende coalesce.

I haven't always liked spring,

but adore this one: the red

of tulips I'd forgotten, how light

leaves' green can be.

Goodbye, God be with you: Adieu.

Claude n'est plus, his wife's letter said.

Barbara

by Jacques Prévert

Remember Barbara
It rained all that day in Brest
And you walked along smiling
Soaking wet   delighted   lit up from inside
In the rain
Remember Barbara
It rained and rained in Brest
And I ran into you on Siam Street
You were smiling
And me   I was smiling too
Remember Barbara
You whom I didn't know
You who didn't know me
Remember
Remember that day nonetheless
Don't forget
A man sheltered himself under a porch
And he cried out your name
Barbara
And you ran towards him in the rain
Dripping wet so pleased your beauty a blossom
And you threw yourself in his arms
Remember that Barbara
And please don't mind if I use the familiar with you
I say "tu" to all those I love
Even if I've only seen them once
I use the familiar with everyone in love
Even if I don't know them
Remember Barbara
Don't forget
That wise and happy rain
On your contented face
Falling on that joyful town
That rain falling on the sea

On the arsenal
On the boat from Ouessant
Oh Barbara
War is such crap
What has become of you
Under this iron rain
Under this rain of fire steel and blood
And the one who held you in his arms
Lovingly
Is he dead has he disappeared or is he still alive
Oh Barbara
It's raining nonstop on Brest
Like it was raining then
But it's not the same now everything ruined
It's a terrible and desolate mourning rain
It's no longer even a storm
Of iron steel and blood
Only clouds
that burst   like dogs dropping dead
Dogs that disappear
On the current that flows from Brest
And who will rot far
So far from Brest
Of which there's nothing left.

Translated by Elizabeth J. Coleman

4.
AND I WANT TO
START AGAIN

I Bring News to My Grandparents
Who Disembarked at Ellis Island 100 Years Ago

When at wharf's end
Ellis Island
appears in view
I tell you

of your two
great great grandchildren
born six days ago
to whom

my husband of forty years—
you've also not met him—
whispered: If you were giraffes,
you'd be running all around by now

To My Husband's Brother Whose Photo Sat over the TV

Lawrence, you're still a blond boy on a bike
as siblings grow gray, grandparents now.
Nephews have been born, one niece has died,
while, Lawrence, you have stayed astride,
neck jutting forward like a bird as you ride
to see what's beyond the corner of the house.
To this day you remain that boy on a bike,
siblings grown gray, grandparents now.

Don't worry about me, Robert, you told my Bob
just a few days before you died,
and stayed forever that country boy.
Don't worry, kiddo, you said to Bob,
cheerful as if you'd not been robbed
of a chance to make a go of life.
I'll be o.k., brother, you reassured Bob
a day or so before you died.

Secret Messages

In a time when people knew what snowsuits were,
she knitted a sweater too small for her child

and thought of her mother's smile, before
the lipstick bled, before the nurse

stole the pearls. She's known
her lover's father longer than she knew

her own, and is running out of memories.
Sometimes snow is blue, sometimes pink,

hardly ever white, she notes, as trees
write their secret messages across the sky,

a glass of red wine shatters on the table,
a spider crawls across the old man's beard.

CELEBRATION

Occupy Wall Street marchers carry hand-scrawled signs,
the leader's gray braid swinging in time to their song.

We lean out our window, cheer them on. Wanting
to be part of something too, we go see a film
about a kid with a fifty-fifty chance.

He's going to be ok, so we head to our favorite
out-door café to celebrate. In all the world, it's just
Bob, me, my bread pudding, his crab cake,

and the waiter, a dead ringer for Kevin Spacey.
Unless you count the guy shouting *fuck you*
joyfully on the sidewalk, whose voice reverberates

down to the end of the block and up
towards our lonely moon.
In New York, you cannot see the stars.

RUMI'S MESSAGE

Rumi says I'm a high-flying bird, my thoughts
mere gnats. But a black hole contains so much
matter packed in, that nothing, not even light,

can keep from being swallowed. I've decided again
never to turn my eyes from injustice or evil: to face them
cheerfully like Tich Nath Hanh or the Dali Lama. But

it's like my pledge to be a vegetarian: Neither lasts
in the face of what I see. And the thing is: they have
all those incarnations to look forward to.

The first time I heard Patsy Cline her voice was smooth,
sad and knowing, like the reflection of a mangrove tree
in a black lagoon, the kind we'd canoe through

in the Okeefenokee. I've always loved mangroves,
palms even more. When we took the train to Florida
at Christmastime, my father kissed the first of us to see

a palm. If only I still dreamed of him; if he were more real
than the man in the letters who drew stick figures to show me
what he'd done that day. Now sometimes my dad and I skip

ahead of the others down the long red carpet
where my grandparents live. We let our index fingers touch
as in a Michelangelo, and we give each other shocks and laugh.

THE SAINT OF LOST THINGS

On Naxos, we climb past hobbled cows
across rocks to the sea; a man along
the path--live goats in satchels,
struggling, on his donkey's sides—
makes an eating motion, leers at me.

Last night I conceived a child
named Athena I lost her in a mountain cove
then found her again at the Chapel
of the Saint of Lost Things

In town, old women chant behind
church curtains or in cigarette kiosks,
whispers intimate as clothes hung out to dry:
men's under-shorts, frayed pajamas.

And there's the local rooster, head colorful
as scarves for sale. He crowed at dawn, unaware
he will appear with goat on the menu tonight.

HOW WHEN MY MOTHER RETURNED FROM EUROPE IN 1931 AND SAW HER OWN MOTHER AT THE DOCK SHE REALIZED HER BROTHER HAD DIED, A TANKA

Nothing would ever be said   and
the elegant black
dress made sense—fashion was her
business after all — but
then mother saw the black stockings

THE DIAGNOSIS

The doctor runs out of the room to call
for help, and I realize: this is what's hovered
overhead like a low-flying chopper.

One snuck up on us at the picnic on Lihou
that day with Yvie who years later
swallowed pills to die. Blue sky unscarred
by clouds, Channel Island cattle silent.
On our blanket butter and jam, tea-bags,
sugar packets purloined from local inns.

Before the 'copter split the sky, the only sound
a yellow-browed warbler's song.

                                     Six months after
the diagnosis, helicopters hover over New York
and neighbors sit outside a blue-awninged
café on a mid-September night—
none of us can bear to be alone.

Dinner With Ellen

I tell her my heart felt wide as the world
at Sunday brunch with my family, and how
I started to say *I can eat all I want*, then realized:

It's my daughter who's pregnant, not I.
Ellen wheels her father around now.
The psychiatrist tells him, *listen to your children,*

and I tell her Bob's having a stress test tomorrow,
which reminds me, If you let time pass, things happen,
like Ellen's brother getting early onset Alzheimer's

and Bob needing a pacemaker. It's good news,
the doctor said—light-headed was a bad symptom.
We talk about an increase in snowy owl sightings

and Bob's having to go to work in a taxi. I married someone
who was kind, she says. I was sick of people who were mean.
Which reminds me how Epictetus scoffed: you'd be saying

a lot worse if you knew me better. We laugh at this ancient
wit, the waiter brings coffee, and Ellen tells me they've resurrected
a 32,000 year-old plant with delicate white flowers.

THE MOUNTAIN HOUSE

Spruces circle my cabin
in a game of ring-a-round-a-rosy,
turning heads slowly
from the mountain towards me.

At dawn the cry
of a lone crow. My
mother calling to me
from the skies. And in the
hoo of an owl
my father . *Do not rush*

to join us, they say. *From
the breaths that were our last,
wait to build your wings.*

THERE ARE TIMES

I imagine I'm the type who'll go
to the mountains alone, pick blackberries
from a bush at twilight, then down to the neighbors
for a drink.
          (I'll have a Hepburn accent, be
rangy like a character from Cheever or Updike.)

Accompanied by a yellow lab or two,
I'll wave to a friend as I come home
to cook an omelet, drink a whiskey, finish
Proust at last, relish sleeping in
pure dark, be up at dawn

to do yoga, have black coffee as the sun
appears, hoping today I'll see a bear, having
only a passing acquaintance with fear,
which I'll determine is a bore.

—THE ONE WITH VIOLETS IN HER LAP, AN ELEGY
After Sappho:

At the funeral her step-son
said   I have an image
of Judy the family's yelling

at one another you know
how nasty these things get   Judy
goes into the next room   sets

a table   white cloth
edged with lace   polished
silver at each place   linen

napkins   a bouquet of calla lilies
tulips roses daisies
she hums to herself then sings aloud

and one by one the whole family
wanders from the room
with the fighting into

Judy's dining room
Someone lights
the candles —Judy is the one
with violets in her lap

AND I WANT TO START AGAIN

I ride backward on the train: face
the guy replacing me
talk about problems that are no longer mine.

I'm a zebra running in the season
of great migration in the Bush. I'm the turkey
spared by the President on Thanksgiving,
the pigeon that didn't get run over by the SUV,
the rat that found the square of bread left
by a homeless man in the subway.

It took moxie to walk away, a colleague says.
How I love that word, born
of a soft drink.
But it wasn't so much moxie talking
as a brush with cancer.

I'd like grandchildren or at least a dog,
though I try to remember that Buddhist idea
that all the dogs on the street are mine
and everybody's, and things don't belong to us.

Then I picture the photo of my children
sitting on the grass with the Eiffel Tower
in the background when we were young
and making dumb mistakes,
and I want to start again.

Elizabeth J. Coleman is the author of *Let My Ears Be Open* (Finishing Line Press, 2013) and *The Saint of Lost Things* (Word Temple Press, 2009), two chapbooks of poems. In 2012, *Proof*, this collection, was a finalist for the University of Wisconsin Press' Brittingham and Pollak prizes. Elizabeth's poetry has been published in the journals *Connecticut Review*, *Raintown Review*, *32 Poems*, *Per Contra*, *Blueline*, and *Peregrine*, among others, and her poems appear in *The Bloomsbury Anthology of Contemporary Jewish American Poetry*, and in the forthcoming *Poetry in Medicine Anthology* to be released by Persea Books. A 2012 recipient of an MFA in Poetry at the Vermont College of Fine Arts, Elizabeth is also an attorney and guitarist. She can be visited on the Web at www.elizabethjcoleman.com.

Acknowledgments

I would like to thank the editors and publishers of the following publications where some of the poems in this volume have appeared or will appear:

32 Poems: "For Nine Months"
Anthology of Jewish American Poetry: "Prayer in Anticipation of a Guitar Recital," "Catskills Love"
The Connecticut Review: "Middlefield"
"J" Journal: "Breathless" (as "Shot")
The Legal Studies Forum: "A Daughter Contemplates Fir Mountain" (as "Fir Mountain"), "Proof," "Illumination," "Admission Against Interest," "George Washington Bridge"
Let My Ears Be Open, Georgetown: Finishing Line Press, 2013: "Prayer in Anticipation of a Guitar Recital," "At a Café Overlooking a Tenth-Century Church in Eril-le-Val, Spain" (as "Near a Tenth-Century Church in Northern Spain"), "Where Exactly Is Heaven in Relation to the Sun," "In Memoriam," "Sometimes I Pass You on the Street," "Elegy for a Father-in-Law," "One Possibility," "A Cup of Tea," "Someone Always Crying in the Dining Room," "The First Time," "Breathless," "19, Avenue Franklin Roosevelt," "The Familiar," "Morning," "The Present," "What Do Women Want," "And I Want to Start Again," "Catskills Love," "Fir Mountain," "The Weight," "Breakfast at Sweet Sue's"
Peregrine: "Secret Messages" (as "The Weight")
Literary Gazette: "The Bamboo in the Garden"
Per Contra: "Annual Physical," "The Gesture," "Google"
Persimmon Tree: "Finally, Justice"
The Phoenicia Times: "A Daughter Looks to Fir Mountain" (as "Fir Mountain")
Umbrella: "Middlefield"
Poetry in Medicine, Persea Books (2014): "The One With Violets in her Lap," "I Want to Start Again"
The Saint of Lost Things. Santa Rosa: Word Temple Press, 2009: "Breathless," "19, Avenue Franklin Roosevelt," "Middlefield," "Gauguin's Words," "The Saint of Lost Things" (as "Kreta") "For nine months," "A Daughter Contemplates Fir Mountain," "The Inheritance"

Still Against War, Poems for Marie Ponsot. Jamie Stern and Nan Hall Lombardi, 2011: "And I Want To Start Again," "Breathless"
Still Against War II: Poems for Marie Ponsot. New York: Jamie Stern and Nan Hall Lombardi, 2012: "Lower Manhattan, September, 2011," "At a Café Overlooking a Tenth-Century Church in Eril-le-Val, Spain" (as "Near a Tenth-Century Church in Northern Spain")
The Yale Journal for Humanities in Medicine, September 2010, yjhm.yale.edu/, "And I Want to Start Again."

The poem "Barbara," is from the collection PAROLES by Jacques Prevert © Editions Gallimard, Paris, 1949, with the permission of the publisher.

Additionally, I cannot thank my poetry teachers enough: Mark Cox, Richard Jackson, Thomas Lux, Marie Ponsot, Natasha Sajé, Betsy Sholl, Lee Slonimsky, Estha Weiner. I also thank my poetry colleagues and mentors who gave me invaluable feedback on these poems, and so much encouragement: Rob Casper, Sharon Israel Cucinotta, Andrea Fry, Lee Gould, Katherine Hastings, the late Daniel Hoffman, Brett Fisher Lauer, Susannah Laurence, Alice Quinn, Gerald Stern, Karen Swenson, Ronald Wallace, Deborah Warren.

S P U Y T E N   D U Y V I L
Meeting Eyes Bindery
Triton
Lithic Scatter